A WORLD TOGETHER

Sonia Manzano
Sesame Street's "Maria"

NATIONAL
GEOGRAPHIC
KiDS

NATIONAL GEOGRAPHIC
WASHINGTON, D.C.

How many **WONDERFUL PEOPLE** do you know?

You know your **FAMILY** and **FRIENDS.**
You know your **NEIGHBORS** and **TEACHERS.**

Did you know there are about **8 BILLION PEOPLE** on the planet?

That's more than you can count in your whole lifetime!

They live on different continents, in different countries.

Do you wonder what kinds of **HOUSES** they live in?

All these people HUG and SHOW LOVE in the same way you do.

They get warmed by the same sun, and sleep under the same stars.

Do you wonder about what people EAT?

Imagine all the different foods you can TASTE.

DUMPLINGS, MEATBALLS, TORTILLAS, BABA GANOUSH, PIZZA.

One thing you can count on: No matter where they're from,

NO KID CAN RESIST DESSERT! Is your tummy rumbling?

And while your **SCHOOL** may be different ...

... your GAMES may be different ...

... your DANCING

may be different ...

... and your ART may be different ...

... isn't it amazing that everyone loves to LEARN and PLAY and MOVE and CREATE?

Other kids might speak a different LANGUAGE from you.

It might sound a little different the first time you hear it.

But you can still share stories.

And isn't it fun to talk with new friends?

Some days you might feel HAPPY or SAD,
EXCITED or WORRIED, GLAD or MAD.

Everyone in the world has felt these feelings.

And when people feel SCARED,

they sometimes forget that deep down we're all the same.

But when they **LAUGH** together, they remember.

And with laughter and love, we bring **A WORLD TOGETHER.**

Isn't that wonderful?

That's because the world is full of wonderful people, JUST LIKE YOU!

WONDERFUL PEOPLE AROUND THE WORLD

Arctic Ocean

CANADA

UNITED KINGDOM

RUSSIA

FRANCE

CROATIA

MONGOLIA

UNITED STATES

SPAIN

GREECE

JAPAN

Pacific Ocean

West Bank

Kashmir

CHINA

MEXICO

British Virgin Islands

EGYPT

PAKISTAN

Puerto Rico

INDIA

Hong Kong

GUATEMALA

MALI

THAILAND

PHILIPPINES

COLOMBIA

CAMBODIA

Pacific Ocean

ECUADOR

SRI LANKA

UGANDA

PAPUA NEW GUINEA

BRAZIL

Atlantic Ocean

TANZANIA

Indian Ocean

MAP KEY

AUSTRALIA

▨ Country where photo was taken

SOUTH AFRICA

• Location of photo

| **U.S.A.** | **U.S.A.** | **Brazil** | **India** | **Greece** | **China** |
| Tetra images RF/Getty Images | Gabriel Bucataru/Stocksy United | The Image Bank/Getty Images | Poras Chaudhary/The Image Bank/Getty Images | Nasos Zovoilis/Stocksy United | Bruno Morandi |

| **South Africa** | **Spain** | **U.S.A.** | **U.S.A.** | **British Virgin Islands** | **Guatemala** | **U.S.A.** |
| Klaus Vedfelt/Digital Vision/Getty Images | Addictive Creatives/Stocksy United | ballyscanlon/Photographer's Choice RF/Getty Images | Getty Images/Tetra images RF | Anya Brewley Schultheiss/Stocksy United | Bruno Morandi | Jaren Wicklund/Alamy Stock Photo |

Philippines
Bruno Morandi

Thailand
Chalit Saphaphak/
Stocksy United

Egypt
Mohamed Abd El Ghany/Reuters

France
Denys Kuvaiev/iStockphoto/
Getty Images

Papua New Guinea
Bruno Morandi

U.S.A.
Peathegee Inc/
Blend Images/Tetra images
RF/Getty Images

Brazil
Yann Arthus-Bertrand/Getty Images

Mongolia
Bruno Morandi

Hong Kong
Lingxiao Xie/Moment Unreleased
RF/Getty Images

U.S.A.
Dmitry Travnikov/500px Plus/
Getty Images

Japan
Eriko Koga/Digital Vision/
Getty Images

U.S.A.
Gabriel Bucataru/Stocksy United

Colombia
andresr/iStockphoto/
Getty Images

United Kingdom
Edward Westmacott/
Alamy Stock Photo

Uganda
Images of Africa/Gallo Images
ROOTS Collection/Getty Images

Sri Lanka
Ami Vitale

Ecuador
Iryna Kurilovych/iStockphoto/
Getty Images

U.S.A.
Aaron Farley/The Image Bank/
Getty Images

Croatia
Jelena990/iStockphoto/Getty Images

Mexico
Juanmonino/iStockphoto/
Getty Images

Tanzania
Sohadiszno/iStockphoto/
Getty Images

India
Lori Epstein/National Geographic Image Collection

Russia
Bruno Morandi

Cambodia
Bruno Morandi

South Africa
Trevor Adeiline/Caiaimage/Getty Images

U.S.A.
Lou Jones/Lonely Planet Images/Getty Images

Mali
haidara01/CFP/Moment Select/
Getty Images

**Kashmir,
Pakistan/India**
Ami Vitale

U.S.A.
Ami Vitale

China
Bo Bo/Stocksy United

Spain
Carol Yepes/Moment RF/
Getty Images

U.S.A.
Cavan Images RF/Getty Images

Canada
Ami Vitale

U.S.A.
Staff Sgt. Jorge Intriago/U.S. National Guard

**West Bank,
Palestinian territories**
Ami Vitale

Australia
Andrew Thurtell/E+/Getty Images

Puerto Rico
SuperStock/Alamy Stock Photo

Above, left to right: My mother, Isidra Rivera Manzano, in Puerto Rico; my sister, Aurea Andino, in Puerto Rico; my mother and great-aunt on the roof of our building in the Bronx, New York City. **Below:** Me with my furry *Sesame Street* friend Rosita.

Hola!

I want to tell you about two photos that fascinated me when I was a kid growing up in the Bronx. They were of my mother and older sister in Puerto Rico. You see, at that time I had never been to Puerto Rico, so of course I was curious about where my mother and sister had come from.

In the photos they are nicely dressed but posing in front of crude houses. The shacks they stood in front of could not have been more different from the buildings we lived in in the Bronx. Those black-and-white photos gave me a glimpse into my mother's and sister's lives before I was born.

When I finally visited Puerto Rico for the first time, I understood my mother even more, in both profound and superficial ways. I understood her desire to grab the U.S.A.'s invitation to work on the mainland, and after seeing the turquoise blue Caribbean Sea for the first time, I understood why she painted the kitchens and bathrooms in all the tenements we ever lived that very color!

On that visit, I was thrilled that everyone understood my Spanish, even though it was sprinkled with so much English. I began thinking about how Puerto Ricans born on the island, like my mother and older sister, were the same—and different—from Puerto Ricans born on the mainland, like me.

Fast-forward several years to my role as Maria on *Sesame Street*. There are many reasons I loved being on *Sesame Street,* but a major one was that it is seen and welcomed all over the world. I believe it succeeds because all people share a love of learning and often laugh at the very same things!

In a divided world, multicultural understanding and tolerance become more important than ever. This book gives a glimpse into the everyday lives of people from around the globe. I hope it encourages lively conversations about shared experiences and the fascinating similarities—and differences—that connect us all.

Gracias!
Sonia Manzano

TO THE CHILDREN OF PUERTO RICO—SM

Text Copyright © 2020 Sonia Manzano

Compilation Copyright © 2020 National Geographic Partners, LLC

Published by National Geographic Partners, LLC, Washington, DC, 20036. All rights reserved. Reproduction of the whole or any part of the contents without written permission from the publisher is prohibited.

NATIONAL GEOGRAPHIC and Yellow Border Design are trademarks of the National Geographic Society, used under license.

Designed by Brett Challos

Author's Acknowledgments
This book is a collaborative effort, and so I extend heartfelt thanks to editor Marfé Delano for her guidance, photo director Lori Epstein for finding the most delightful images to make my words hit home, designer Brett Challos for putting the words and photos together so beautifully, Ebonye Gussine Wilkins for her cultural insight on all aspects of this book, and to my agent Jennifer Lyons for her constant support. Of course, I would be remiss not to thank my family, Richard and Gabriela Reagan, without whom nothing is possible. Abrazos to everyone! May the sentiment in this book live on.

Photo Credits
Personal photos courtesy of the author.
Photo of Sonia Manzano at Sesame Street © (2020) Sesame Workshop®. Sesame Street® and associated characters, trademarks and design elements are owned and licensed by Sesame Workshop.
All Rights Reserved.

Library of Congress Cataloging-in-Publication Data

Names: Manzano, Sonia, author.
Title: A world together / Sonia Manzano.
Description: Washington, DC : National Geographic Kids, 2020. | Audience: Ages 4-8 | Audience: Grades K-1
Identifiers: LCCN 2019034714 | ISBN 9781426337383 (hardcover) | ISBN 9781426337390 (library binding)
Subjects: LCSH: Communities--Juvenile literature. | Cultural pluralism--Juvenile literature.
Classification: LCC HM756 .M365 2020 | DDC 307--dc23
LC record available at https://lccn.loc.gov/2019034714

Printed in Malaysia
20/QRM/1